Give Me a Holler

Chelsie Blair Nunn

Disclaimer

This book is not intended to stigmatize, attack, or represent any individual church or group. This book is not a representation of all church/religious experiences or expressions of church/religion. This book is not intended to perpetuate any hateful opinions of any religion, group, class, region, gender, sexuality, race, etc. Depictions of individuals or groups of people are not specific to any real living or deceased human being, and any resemblance to the communities or individuals described within the book is entirely coincidental. However, if you do relate to this book, give me a holler.

To all the wild dogs

Contents

Our Tour Bus

now normally I would say
huffing glue is bad for a person
unless you need a deeper
connection with your mother

she's beautiful when she laughs
high on those green carpeted
walls rolling around
in an old Opryland bus
repurposed for the Lord's work

we were drunk on carpet glue
after we formed a gospel band
needed a way to get to holy places
the rural south
churches with no plumbing

only wild packs of dogs

Bunk Beds

stop lights were the problem
with bunk beds in a gospel tour bus
there were no seatbelts
carpet burn sometimes got
my whole body ha
I rolled all the way up to
my father the bus driver
gazed at him from my position on the floor
under the swirling door handle—
the kind I think of when soldiers come
home Rosa Parks birthed out as
a new woman I'm not quite a woman
I do have a father
he drove an old Opryland bus to
churches in the woods

Womb Renovation

take me back to being seven years old
buzzed on carpet glue
renovating a broken-down theme park
bus that once carried people
away from their parked cars and
closer to joy

we were inside her and she was
carpeted green—green fuzzies in
my hair as we laughed ourselves silly

I have a body
I had a body then
it was warm
my eyes cried from chemicals and from
being ludicrous with my mother

this is where I go when
I imagine coming from a woman
we were inside her
a new mother called joy
on her chest crying
this is why people do drugs

Prometheus

if you've never smelled like kerosene
then we don't have much in common
seen a mother lather lanolin on her swollen
breasts after feeding an infant then
it's alright but I know we ain't cut from
the same cloth as they say quilted by a
different hand a different fabric stretched
underneath a walnut tree out in the country
square by square someone who couldn't
see very well in their old age probably
wore a thimble like banjo picks
metal on metal into something soft
Frankenstein–like ten mamaws around a loom
that's who made me sewed me into this pattern
gorgeous but unhinged geometrically
little knotted strings make up my spine
ten rough knuckles bent to tie bent to thread
the eyes of needles patchwork of freckles
hay stuck to batting where they let my
legs touch the ground

Cumberland Gap Tunnel 1996

they blasted a hole in that mountain
so we could get to the Wal-Mart Supercenter
they constructed a tunnel that took about 1 minute
12 seconds to drive through
I know on account of holding my breath
drew a long inhale of Tennessee
upon entering a $280 million dollar
laceration in the Appalachian Range
enough to make my tongue tingle
my eyes involuntarily cried
hyphenated rows of lights
we swallowed laughter in gulps
before exhaling Kentucky
with a desperate gasp
crazy how you can be in one
state and then another in such a

short time

Check Check 1-2-3

check red check white check blue
stripes on the side of our Opryland bus
I hear the colors of Old Glory never fade but
the sun had done a hot number on them
we were American we brought the gospel
to people of the deep woods
Saturdays and Sundays packed
with subwoofers and microphone cases
black egg crates like cradles
kept the equipment safe during
travel—violent stops at red lights
no match for these bad boys
clickety clack closures all over those boxes
meant nothing could harm the investment
my folks had made to live this humble life
microwave bolted to the cabinet everything bolted
we were like sailors
we were sailors
the ship swayed so did our things
so did we sway
this is where I learned the word *reverb*
you must hear your own self singing
          your own self singing
He leadeth me O blessed tho't
yo ho yo ho and a bottle of rum

T 1102

Bloodline

oh we hugged those crooked roads in our
Opryland bus sun-dappled isn't
a good enough word for the strobing
sunlight riddling pane after pane
limitless thuds on the goofy rooftop
from branches that worshiped our top-heavy
freedom to croon around the Clinch
Mountains touching the hem of our dreams
branches that witnessed my ancestors
tuck themselves a mystery inside their cabins
farmed each blade of the Sycamore land
darkened their hands with soil that
bequeathed green beans in Mason jars
they were real people and they
were my people strange to the outside
world and strange even unto themselves
I heard you can't see the forest for the trees
what if the trees see you instead
what if they know who I am
queer in the peculiar way
the country way my whole family a tin can of corn
rolled down the valley on its side sister
bloodline of fears that swished our veins
kept us concealed away in the woods the ridge
no matter how far we drove that bus that river
it was only us and our holler that barn that curve
churches Lord I pray our souls to keep that cool spring
that forest of trees those mountains that valley

The Outhouse

vault toilets always scared
the shit out of me
total darkness is perpetual if you
look the hole in its beady eyes
sometimes bees were in there
other creatures made homes in
pit toilets I'm sure of it
my mamaw always said

plumbing was a luxury
cost money required
proximity to waste management
these places were so far in the sticks
they don't have street view
on Google Maps even now
it's a city thing you wouldn't get it
no it's a country thing you wouldn't get it

take yourself outside a church
walk some twenty yards to a shack
look into the vaulted eyes of your mother
stand over the perpetual darkness
the urge to urinate is greater than
whatever lurks in that black hole
probably snakes
close your eyes
hold fast to her lifted biceps

now my great-grandmother
was bitten in the leg by a copperhead
when she stepped on a log in the yard
took the ambulance more than an hour
on account of the curvy roads

Water Damage

church basements all smelled like ghosts
at least they did in the country
slathered with moldy hymnals
shot straight up the nostrils
my cerebrum inhaled hidden
ailments unwilling hearts

prayer rooms were always in
these haunted cellars
wooden kneeling benches
sprays of fake flowers
one isolated altar sick with red light

maybe we all roll out occasionally
our bunk beds jolt at red lights
kneel to pray on the softest green carpet
unwrap a Jolly Rancher
in the basement of a church
to pass the time

While My Parents Sang

call me a lyrical architect
constructing houses out of hymnals
I sat in pews by myself
an overpopulated bathtub
soaked in perfume cologne perfume etc.
puddled tears from everyone crying
amen hallelujah amen etc.
so much screaming
bodies crammed together in fragrant
raucous heat Wrigley's Juicy Fruit
stuck in everyone's hair
juicy fruit heads on the floor
juicy fruit heads thrown backwards
juicy fruit heads wrapped around
other juicy fruit heads

I hated putting on that red coat
when it was time to go

LEY'S
JUICY FRUIT
CHEWING GUM
THE GUM WITH THE FASCINATING FLAVOR

It Could Have Been Worse

first greet the pastor
prop the chapel doors open
park the bus in a convenient place
hands on hips
survey the amount of
equipment to be unloaded
get to it

this was before I was ripped with
muscles and brawn too small to help
more liability than assistance
I wandered outside
rambled around the outhouse
hoping to find an animal but
scared to death I actually would
step on a snake
you know the ones
supposedly handled during service

it wasn't snakes
that chased me down a gravel road
teeth snarled wet with rage

no—it was a wild pack of dogs
country dogs are just different
than city ones and so are
gravel roads that lay out like tongues
over miles of rolling limestone hills

Okay the First Time I Ever Saw a Real Snake

my father was a dang hero
coming in hot with his rifle
can you get him for us?
he's eating up our chickens
oh Mylanta he was a big boi
tucked away in a limestone cave
I could see his slick profile
between boulders and chicken feathers
he was just making an honest living

honesty by the way is a sacrifice some of us make

it can get you straight up murdered
in the sunshine beside a waterfall
could be the most beautiful day
the one you die on—
looking into the barrel of a shotgun
Lord I know it's something awful to say
but it's how big black beautiful snakes
live in Rural Appalachia
there's always a small child watching you die
sees your body slink in the burly hand of a pretty nice father
looks at your honest blood drip between his honest fingers

a little kid recently told me I am
a good person for liking snakes
now that I think about it I suppose he meant
some of us see ourselves in snakes
some of us see ourselves in our father's hand

Native Fauna

it's illegal to kill any snake
even with a shovel
especially the venomous ones
my mother used to have shovels for
hands that chopped the heads off
anything that slithered by her
especially anything at all
I reckon a lot of mothers have
these hands that kill snakes
protecting us from our own
flickering tongues
people are proud to put an end to danger
especially mothers
they hold it up by its tail on social media

I've heard of people who pay no mind to fines
they are rich with mothers and unaffected
although a shovel is a curious weapon for
ending a long line of scales
unless you need a lengthy handle
a butcher knife from the kitchen is too short
would place her within striking distance of
a quick and reasonable response

Pastures 1997

everyone who grew up around
electric fences knows how to
get especially close to something
without getting close enough to die
how to extend yourself with a twig
or a leaf and move in slowly towards
a barb that hums
touch it without touching it
enter a magnetic field by proxy
feel the jolt from the wire to our fingertips
a pulse that travels to a 6,000 volt gaze
that somehow tells our mothers:
we will never die we will never live

now my mamaw
was sitting on the toilet when a big
black snake fell from the ceiling onto
the floor in front of her feet
coiled up in fear the both of them
neither could get a word out

This One is a Waterfall

the only time I ever
felt safe within the sanctuary of
a church was when I was being
chased by a pack of wild dogs
holy home plate
safe under the blankets
nighttime with the ghosts standing all around
the feeling of having a proper basement
during a tornado—that's the relief of running
inside those propped doors
my parents already unloaded
equipment for the altar
plugging in cords here and there
they turned to see my
hands outstretched to Heaven
eyes turned to the sky
backed against the foyer wall
beads of sweat trickling down my face
or tears I'm not sure

The Auction

my grandmother's stack cakes
raised more money than any Girl Scout
standing in front of a grocery store
could ever dream of at auction
during the church fall festival
a preacher would hold her cakes high
dripping with sweat and apple butter
Lord, he had to be strong because
them cakes was heavy
he always stood high up on the concrete stairs
outside the old schoolhouse's green doors
bid calling a *yip* as the congregation fought over
stacks and stacks of sugar
yip my grandmother smiled in her creaking
lawn chair under the quilters' tent
I could feel her pride flow down the creek to me
the one wearing overalls because I was a
tomboy and could get away with it
I reckon it was a tough battle to
get out of wearing those dresses and bonnets
finally trudge knee-deep into the water and
fish what I called *slop* outta the creek bed
flung it over the bank with a long sycamore
branch *yip* I could hear them selling like
the hot cakes they really were
with every pile of slop on the creek bank

I wiped my brow with my red handkerchief
yip nothing good is free nothing good is
easy that slop wouldn't scoop itself
now would it

I Go Back

I take people to the countryside these days
someone dear to me in the passenger seat
glosses over the limestone shards
poking out of the grassy green carpet

I was baptized in that cement pool
fills up with creek water when
you lift that metal thing
it was really cold
my mother sewed a white dress for me
it was really white
against the dark water

I hold my breath against these truths
I baptize myself in my own dark waters
no one sews me dresses anymore

now my grandmother would always say
Tweeter stay outta that garage
cause snakes like to hide in the rafters
those hot days of summer I'd still
sneak to see for myself
if I could catch a rattler hanging
up by the Radio Flyer sled
how many times I thought its pull rope
was the tail end of something special

Honestly

it was the speaking in tongues
the lady swallowed by pink satin
she was a bubblegum angel at the pulpit
illuminated under those bright lights
sanguine sticky injection of Holy Spirit
Heavenly birth plopped her down on that altar
warm uterus of the church
pregnant with hundreds of people
all laying hands on each other
because there was nowhere else to put them

she was talking about her brother

she was speaking in tongues
I guess some of us are born with more than one

syrup of kindness
horizontal drip of language
my ears are stacked full of sugar
I am baptized but
I only know one tongue

Pocket Squares

my father's face was slick
with salty redness singing acapella
he used a pitch pipe to conjure
correct notes like magic from the air
while I played it like a flute
oblivious to its purpose
I just knew it was important to him

I forgave him for his flushed warmth
he was in a three-piece suit after all
so was everyone

red
wet
loud

it was not quiet inside the womb
it was hot and soaked inside there
everyone seemed to be yelling
their ink pens went flying as they jumped and
shouted wiping their brows with kerchiefs
their pockets were always full of candy
they knelt in front of my rosy father
cried butterscotch onto the carpet

I'll Wear Real Versace One Day

I imagined being the church custodian
after the parade of kneeling bodies
passed through the aisles shaking hands
dropping candies from their squeezed pockets
digging for more in their purses
wrappers on pews
paper airplanes on the floor
decorated floats all congregated
out in the parking lot smoking cigarettes

walking away from those flamboyant poofs
shoulder pads the height of prayers
I'd amble towards the empty sanctuary
vacuum cleaner in one hand
broom in the other
trash bag tied to my belt loop
my suit was always different
I wore overalls with a folded bandana
hanging from my back pocket
I wiped my sweat like the candied men except
bent down before the shiny Juicy Fruit wrappers
collected them as if they could be recycled
melted down and forged into silver chains
knockoff Versace coins around my neck
people wouldn't just call me a sinner
they would call me a sweet fancy one

now my uncle would always say
the cave over there in the cow
pasture is a rattlesnake nest
I ended up hiding there when
the herd chased me once
I guess all the snakes were asleep

The Quarter Trick

gospel conventions could happen anywhere
the high school the college gymnasium
of course the church
they were long and boring as a track meet
for a kid like me
I would do my usual wandering about
radiant harmonies filled those spaces
while I read the graffiti in bathroom stalls
Jeremy + Sonja 4ever in Sharpie

I studied the cigarettes in dispensers
those machines had the shiniest knobs
I'd ever seen in my life
ugh I wanted to turn them so badly

occasionally someone would pay me mind
entertain me for one set
always hard plastic chairs for hours
they'd take advantage of my innocence
hide a shiny quarter behind my ear
turn the knob and make it vanish
the way only old men can do

he taught me that quarter trick
but I could never hide
the grooved parts between my fingers

The Oasis 1998

my dad always said that little bar
somewhere between our house and well
nothing else really
called The Oasis was the one Garth Brooks
sang about when he mentioned having friends in low places
I believed him because I wanted to feel famous for something
other than gospel and the word ain't
I wanted to believe that a country music superstar would
drown his own sorrows in a place I knew
where the pizza was actually pretty good
the beer was maybe the coldest I ever drank
where we all said *fur* instead of *for*
because that short ŏ was still a little too long for us
even those of us who have made it out
yearn to pronounce a preposition
we climb with open mouths just to slip on down
back into the valley that raised us

In the Valley

religion left the price tags on
me I'm well aware of how much
it cost I often think back to walking
down the aisle to sell my soul
away to the Lord the Lamb of God
a baby sheep in the pasture
I fed it Jesus I fed it
but it ain't grow'd up the way
it was supposed to no
I swear *e'en death's cold wave I will not flee*
still tis' God's hand that
requires exact change
palm held outward in expectation
exaltation won't break
a hunny dollar bill for nothing
night sweats about redemption
day doesn't worry a lick

On the Road

gumball machines mean we aren't home
we are at the mall or the auto repair shop
we have nails in our tires
they are flat to their bones
flop down the road on those flimsy knobs
we call this a state of being–it's more of a life
we are hungry and out of quarters
chewing gum starves us
when we need we need
crackers from the glove compartment of our mother's sedan
we are taking care of you
the mechanic blows these words at us
tiny pink bubbles pop against his tongue
a lackluster breeze of competency fills the waiting room
we are hungry and out of quarters
a nail isn't home in a tire so we're here for a plug
here it is—a greasy steering wheel protective paper on the floorboards
the sticky residue of someone who doesn't care to feed us

now my father answered a call
about some old telephone poles
ready to be cut up and hauled off
I went to help him that day
the blazing sun on white gravel
I ain't ever seen so many snakes
tumble out of logs like that
with every tooth of the chainsaw
the day smelled like tar
runaway ribbons around my feet
all too terrified to be scared
the dust and smoke made it difficult
for my father to see me so surrounded

PLEN T PAK
WRIGLEY'S
Big Red
CINNAMON GUM
17 STICKS

Is It Just Me

in the pews
basement prayer rooms
all the hollers
outhouses
gymnasium hallways
bizarre spiral staircase
in the local high school
bus bunk beds
running from dogs
listening to the singing
learning magic tricks
from old men
turning the shiny cigarette knobs
watching people cry
walking around the altar
shaking hands
shaking my hand
shaking shaking
shaking piñatas onto the floor
scrounging les bonbons
hoarding it for later
Versace isn't real
it doesn't exist here
the shiniest objects are wrappers and knobs here
cigarette butts on the ground here
after the weekly parade

litter is $1G away from glitter
I am $1G away from owning
something real
from being real

Cassette Tape

I pretended to shave my legs with a Hot Wheels car
in the bathtub like my mother
little white plops of shaving cream
clouds floating in a milky sky
CDs weren't a thing yet
so I had a Looney Tunes version of the Beatles
it was cool but I only liked one song
                    she loves you
yeah yeah yeah but she also
shaved me down to nothing
hot wash rag on her breasts
kept the warmth close to herself
while I considered her smooth leg the most
beautiful thing I had ever seen
my chin rested angrily on the cold edge
soapy bubbles formed to her triangular lap
she closed her eyes in that same way
when she sang into the microphone
when she really meant it
when she really got it right
I'll never forget the oversized blue-green blazer
she wore on the cover of her first and only album

YouTube Taught Me Banjo in My Twenties

I learned how to care for a dog
when I was 26 years old
my significant other at the time
showed me how to love an animal
you might find in a fence post hole
or the grocery store parking lot in the rain
it's not the sort of thing the country was
particularly good at—loving animals this way
at least not when I was younger
most of the dogs I saw
were free from care
they were wild and full of fleas
don't get me wrong they had human homes
they just didn't belong there
they belonged outside with the other wild ones
coyotes at night ticks in the daytime
sunny grass in the meadow
chasing bunnies or groundhogs

the country was pretty good at music
but it never taught me a lick
didn't raise me like that
to join my own gospel band
build out my own tour bus with bunks
no one held me in their lap
put my fingers on the frets
I reckon I wasn't strong enough then

The Iron Furnace 2006

the strange thing about the Cumberland Gap is
once you're there you don't even realize it
it's a sideways glance between Middlesboro, KY and
Harrogate, TN the last pound of the hammer
the one that sinks the nail head into the grain
you find yourself suddenly squinting upward
towards a large pile of sandstone they called a furnace
that smelted tons and tons of iron ore in the 1800s
I gave an oral presentation on this in college once
and received the following feedback:

 you sound like the coal miner's daughter

oh the heat from that furnace hit the back of my ears
bellows inflated within me a redness I never knew
whether to be flattered that Loretta Lynn and I
had something in common or to package it all up
ship myself off down the Powell River to a
bigger city where unrefined metals become nicer things
my glowing embers smelted the memory of eating KFC
with my mamaw on the big rock behind that furnace
how we called it Chicken Rock because it was special
how the roots of the trees held our Cokes while we laughed
while we carried on about clear cool spring water
how steam billowed into the energy to produce
massive amounts of riches we would never see

I Really Hate the Cold

when I blow a matchstick out
I go right to the Museum of Appalachia
wassail the week before Christmas
stewing in a big cast iron caldron
cedar or gum timbers
giving their lives for the human condition of
being cold and celebratory in December
one hundred years ago isn't even that long
just ask my house
for God's sake it was warmed in the
winter by a woodfire stove
growing up I helped my father fell those trees
split the wood myself
stacked it into a massive wall
threw unripe walnuts at it in a fit of anger
just breaking something reminded me I'm an animal
fruits cracked against the open wounds my father and I
sliced somewhere in the forest of Tennessee
healing sometimes means burning your cuts

now sometimes I do need
a god or a mother to pray to
days when the sandbags are soaking

Sunday Morning

god this room smells like mac n cheese
someone get your grandma out of the kitchen
tell her to sit down for a minute
take care of herself for once
put her feet up on an ottoman
someone comb her silver hair with love
she'll show you her closed eyelids
her smile will sink into a limp expression
an exhale of fried green tomatoes of sausage patties
draining on a paper towel after the pan
you won't understand her gratitude when
she says she's never complained not
a day in her whole life not ever
it will be the truth and it will be too much
her gaudy jewelry will fold into her wrinkled
neck her open-heart surgery scar mere inches
below the nape of her gown
she doesn't smell like Olay
she is earth and oil she is a hot rag under
the faucet her hands wringing like big
snakes in the meadow you see beyond
the kitchen window sit down sit down
sit down for a minute and rest

ROOTLESS

a houseless man stands at the entrance to
my neighborhood holding a beer can
he sits under the overpass daily
guarding his purple Huffy mountain
bike that gets the job done
he's there every time I make a right turn
at the stop sign with sunglasses on
he looks cool in his denim jacket
for all I know he could be a thief
he might have killed a man once
definitely a liar because we all are liars
someone from his underpass pack yells
hello at him and he raises his arms to the Heavens
cheers to God with his beer

once he was holding a sign that said **ROOFLESS**
I thought it said **ROOTLESS**
the coyotes loudly sing him lullabies at night
I know we all have mothers

all mothers don't sing but mine did
so did my father
they sang into the vaulted toilets
sang away the outhouse creatures
they sang the chewing gum right out of the pockets of
worshippers on hundreds of altars
they turned the shiny knobs on cigarette machines
made quarters disappear behind ears
they wore three-piece suits on their album cover
I never saw a snake inside a church but
eventually learned to run with the wild dogs outside
tell the difference between sweat and tears
adore the reverb of my own voice
when I say I am not rootless

The Barn

I'm trying to remember the word barn
eight years old maybe a loft where I ate
my first Nutty Buddy ice cream in a soggy
cone sitting on a tight bale of hay with
my cousin and a small white minifridge
above the kind of dirt you only see in barns
surrounded by the kind of weathered wood
you only see in barns lariat ropes made from
hemp itchy on a nail the memory itself hairy
I'm thirty-five now and with you in the rain
watching a small stream form
a cantilever barn that also happens to be
a landmark instead of property my family owns
I'm struggling to explain what it means to be in this
barn with you I want to eat ice cream except
I want it to be my first time again
except I want it to be with you
laughing as we climb a shoddy ladder
we could certainly fall to our deaths but we don't
consider the possibility of anything other than dessert
the surprise chocolate at the end

Kind of Paradise

the entire countryside is my mother
my father a hidden spring down the road
that house on the hill is haunted
I am haunted by the time someone
didn't understand how the bend in the creek
is a caress to my tired shoulder
how the crunchy meadow grasses
mow the ringing in my ears to a dull hum
my cradle overturned by a flood in the barn
the day my grandmother wrapped her vines
around my aching stomach
she grew and grew there
roots in my sallow gut
the sweetest hush from my coyote siblings
the ridge is full of my blood
when I cry it's only the smell of wildflowers
simmering in the hot holler sun
that brings me back to this dry truth
I get my eyes from the tobacco fields and
my suspicious smile from one hundred
little blue skinks on the bleached woodpile

I am a Hay Bale at Night

even the lighthouse spends time in the dark
even the lighthouse pauses in black solitude
    between cycles
even the lighthouse looks away from what's right
what's moral to spend time away from the glossy stare
of the ocean of the needy helpless uncertain worried
cruise yachts or cargo ships or whatever is coming in that day
Jesus Christ can't ya'll just give me a minute
this job is relentless
being perched on a rocky shoreline hurts
listen I'm flattered and I would be lying if I said I didn't like it
    to be needed to be helpful in some way
it's just that I crave the resin charm resting on her collarbone
her cigarette no her hands no her knowledge of
astrology so casual on a Friday *mistaken for a scorpio*
I ain't no lighthouse and I've never been mistaken for a scorpio
I'm a cerulean bale of hay clad in yellow
heavy in a field of red pressing my full blue weight
into the ground dreaming of light dreaming of dark
dreaming of slick oil in a metal bucket
carried up a vertical mile of stairs only to
burn this whole nervous field to a crisp

Junk Drawer Prayer

O' holy establishment of acceptance
chalice of celebration this is the body
my whole real estate of being
it's all I have to cover in Dolce & Gabbana
I eat from ornamental plates of inclusion
walls drip with golden contentment
does it please you?
my online shopping carts are full
pockets empty of misery
I desire but do not spite that I'm not royalty
I eat beans from a can
pretend they are decadent and they are
I came from a can and I am decadent
kneel at the altar of gratitude
give thanks for a bottle opener when you need it
don't use your teeth to do a job
made for a tool

now I sit only sit sit sit by a pond
the labor of telling another person
what a damn frog sounds like
stretches me to the edge of my southern drawl
my banjo appears in my hands
the scar on my forearm from
picking Blackberry Blossom
my tattoo of a wasp
reminds me to do nothing

We All Want a Mother

what you want from your mother is her tongue
slowly rolling over the candied coating of
yes I love you without reason

savors a sweetness she's never known
her mouth holds the shape of
a hug that is happy to see you

a rough green snake stretches from the
brambles of her confusion to
greet you eyelevel
his bright hue blinds you momentarily
reality licks you
down to your solitude
a core of ember yet to flame

two reeds clang together at once
the wind is a cruel magician

Church Hymnal

Give Me a Holler

I am a hair split at one end
I am fabulous in a field of strawberries
I am rooted in the dirt of someone's head
I have taken every one of you
to the top of that hill
where my sweet mamaw lies
we have all captured the same photograph
on our cell phones
the valley below has on its spring jacket
the clouds don't know any better
we didn't all eat the fried chicken
because some of us are
limited by diet or religion
whatever you call it
KFC is no church
the valley is no Heaven
although when they talk about Heaven
it sounds like they're talking about
this place where I grew up
candy carpeted hymns
fallen from the pockets of our fathers

now there ain't nothing scarier
than staring a copperhead in its eyes
unless you look at it
like it's a sweet thing

Notes about the Artwork

1. The front & back cover artwork is an original painting by Chelsie Blair Nunn.

Title: XX True Crime XX
Medium: Acrylic on panel
Size: 24" x 24"
Photographic documentation by Lauren Farkas

2. Illustrations throughout the book are original paintings and color photographs by Chelsie Blair Nunn.

Medium: Acrylic on Duralar & 35mm photography
Size: 4" x 6"
Photographic documentation by Lauren Farkas

Other Notes

Bradbury, William B. (composer) and Gilmore, Joseph H. (author) (1991). "He Leadeth Me" [sheet music]

Tennessee: Broadman & Holman Publishers (original work published 1862). Lyrics from "He Leadeth Me" appear in "Check, Check, 1-2-3" in line 29 & "In the Valley" lines 10 & 11.

Blackwell, D., & Lee, E. (1990). "Friends in Low Places" [Recorded by G. Brooks]. On *No Fences* [Album].

Capitol Nashville. The poem "The Oasis 1998" references lyrics from "Friends in Low Places" in line 16.

Lennon, John & McCartney, Paul (songwriters). "She Loves You" (1963) performed by The Beatles. Lyrics from "She Loves You" appear in the poem "Cassette Tape" in lines 9 & 10.

Acknowledgements

Early versions of "Our Tour Bus," "Bunk Beds," and "Womb Renovation" first appeared in *Bus Stop!*

An early version of "On the Road" first appeared in *Foglifter Press*

"YouTube Taught Me Banjo in My Twenties" first appeared in *Saturnalia '21*

Early versions of "Check Check 123" and "While My Parents Sang" first appeared in *Tofu Ink Arts Press*

An early version of "I'll Wear Real Versace One Day" was previously self-published on *Vocal*, and first appeared in *Tofu Ink Arts Press*

An early version of "This One is a Waterfall" first appeared in *805 Lit + Art*

An early version of "Kind of Paradise" first appeared in *Grim & Grisly*

An early version of "Okay, the First Time I Ever Saw a Real Snake" first appeared in *Quibble Lit*

Early versions of "Junk Drawer Prayer," "Kind of Paradise," and all the untitled snake micropoems first appeared in *Sweet Things* printed by *Shalperta Press*

"Sunday Morning" first appeared in *Denver Quarterly*

"Prometheus" first appeared in *the Ana*

Thank You

to my parents for following their passions, which exposed me to culture and traditions that formed my perception of the world. This experience allowed me to fully engage with the countryside where I grew up, and without it, I would have sorely missed out on a rich, albeit complex, education.

to Anna and Carla for encouraging me to embrace, celebrate, and write about my childhood.

to Lauren Farkas for photographically documenting my artwork with love.

to Dr. Hannah Alpert-Abrams and Shalperta Press for printing the *Sweet Things* zine with love.

to my hairstylist Alyse for making me look confidently fresh for the past decade.

to my dog Loose Boo Boo for being soft and brown.

to all my teachers.

Land Acknowledgement

The land portrayed in this book is part of the traditional territory of the Tsalagi peoples (now Eastern Band of Cherokee Indians, Cherokee Nation of Oklahoma, and United Keetoowah Band of Cherokee Indians), Tsoyahá peoples (Yuchi, Muscogee Creek), and Shawnee peoples. I would like to recognize my native, black, and mixed-race ancestors who farmed this land and continued an oral tradition of story-telling, which I am now participating in as a result of their fortitude.